Hare Publishing.

DEDICATION

To the Victim:

Don't let other peoples opinions, perceptions and behaviours define the person you are or the person you want to become.

To the Bully:

Blowing out other peoples candles, does not make yours shine brighter... Light your own!

To the Bystander:

If you turn a blind eye, watch or walk away to the bullying, to the victim you are as bad as the bully! Stand up and say no!

To all those who Bully; may you be forgiven.

To all those who have been Bullied; may you learn to

forgive.

These things are not okay!

Written and Illustrated

By

Nettie Forsyth

A 'Bully' is a person who harms another person on purpose, intentionally, doing it with enjoyment and knowing, controlling their behaviours.

The 'Bully' forgets or has not learnt this causes someone else to be sad or scared, to have emotional distress.

These things are not okay!

A 'Bully' can come in all shapes, sizes, and ages. They can be biological males, biological females, people from various cultures and ethnicities.

A Bully can be anyone we know, or be a stranger we don't know.

These things are not okay!

A 'Bully' does things over and over again.

They don't listen to STOP, GO AWAY, LEAVE ME ALONE.

These things are not okay!

A 'Bully' likes to bully behind peoples backs and in front of people are not at all the Bully.

A 'Bully' likes to do in front of people who are powerless to help: though they might like to.

These things are not okay!

A 'Bully' is often seen:

As someone trying to make friends, someone who is asserting themselves, someone who is bossy, someone who likes to control others.

Sometimes the people you are asking for help are not listening.

The "Bully" sometimes gets away with it "it's playground fun" "it's just boys being boys" "it's girls being girls" "it's children being children".

These can be excuses so the other person does not have to deal with it!

These things are not okay!

A 'Bully' can be someone who uses physical violence:

Pushing, hitting, thumping, slapping, biting, kicking, stomping on feet, spitting at, pulling at clothes, tripping up, using objects to hurt, tying up, being locked in uncomfortable places, pretending things happened by accident.

These things are not okay!

A 'Bully' can be someone who uses emotional words.

Some can be plain silly and be not you at all; like "stinking pig"

Some can be toilet words "pooh pooh head"

Some can be swearing *+£$%^&*.

Some words can be threatening to you "if you don't do…" then they threaten to hurt you.

Some words can be threatening to others "if you don't do…" then they threaten to hurt someone you love.

Some might be asking you for things; food, money or items.

These things are not okay!

A 'Bully' can be someone who spoils all of your games.

They can be someone who spoils the quiet time with friends.

They can be someone who turns friends against us, by threat or
persuasion.

They can play tricks on you and laugh about it, they can enjoy
humiliating you in front of others.

These things are not okay!

A 'Bully' can be someone who photos you and shares without permission.

A 'Bully' can be someone who gets on social media and makes fun of you behind your back to others.

A 'Bully' sometimes tries to get you at times of embarrassment or tries to get you doing comprising things.

These things are not okay!

A 'Bully' could be someone who sends you unkind texts, messages using social media or emails.

These things are not okay!

A 'Bully' is someone who falsely uses your identity to get things, or to send you things; without you knowing and without your permission.

These things are not okay!

£DUE!

A "Bully" will tell someone that they are the better one, the stronger one, the best one.

The "Bully" might tell someone that they are the weird one, the one that no one likes, the weaker one...

A "Bully" belittles everything about the person to make themselves feel better.

These things are not okay!

1
L

The "Bully" behaviour is sometime relentless. Sometimes it can be everyday, what seems all day and everywhere you go.

The "Bully" behaviour starts to make another person very sad and fearful in what's going to happen next.

Sometimes it get so bad that the person just wants to disappear.

These things are not okay!

12

11

1

10

2

9

3

8

4

7

5

6

The "Bully" forgets friends are for enjoyment and fun.

The "Bully" forgets that friends are suppose to have fun and laughter together, friends are supposed to be happy and smiley together, friends are supposed to be safe within those friendships. The "Bully" forgets good connections are kind and caring towards each other and having great times together.

The "Bully" is not lucky to have those kind of friends.

The "Bully" forgets that Friends say sorry for, their actions, that Friends accidentally hurt each other because they are learning to have relationships and sometimes get it wrong.

The "Bully" forgets an accident is a one off, an accident is not doing it again and again and again and again.

The "Bully" finds it funny and amusing to "Bully", where friends would be sad and say sorry.

These things are not okay!

sorry

The "Bully" uses excuses "it's a clash of personality" Whose personality is it clashing with?

The "Bully" thinks using people's differences against them is okay.

Because Hair colour is different, because they wear glasses to help their sight, because they come from a different country, because they eat different food, because their culture and ethnicity is different, because they are a biological girl, because they are a biological boy, because you can have stuff and they can't, because someone dresses differently, because they learn differently, because someone smells differently....

The "Bully" forgets that difference is really important... it makes us who we are!

The "Bully" forgets that we all think differently, we all like different as well as the same, we can act differently, we believe in different things.

The "Bully" forgets that we are individuals.

These things are not okay!

Child on Child bullying is abuse and it's not okay.

Adult on Child bullying is abuse and it's not okay.

Child on Adult bullying is abuse and it's not okay,

Adult on Adult bullying is abuse and it's not okay.

Adult on Animal bullying is abuse and it's not okay.

Child on Animal bullying is abuse and it's not okay.

Any abuse to another person or animal is not okay.

These things are not okay!

The "Bully" gets away with abuse to another person.

Because people get too sad to stop it!

Because people get too fearful to stop it!

Because people start to believe the "Bully".

Because people ask the wrong people for help

or don't ask for help at all.

The "Bully" forgets people can tell and ask for help again and again.

The "Bully" does not want you to get help.

So they tell you it will get worse if you do.

But the 'Bully' forgets the person needs the bullying to stop and its not okay to not tell!

These things are not okay!

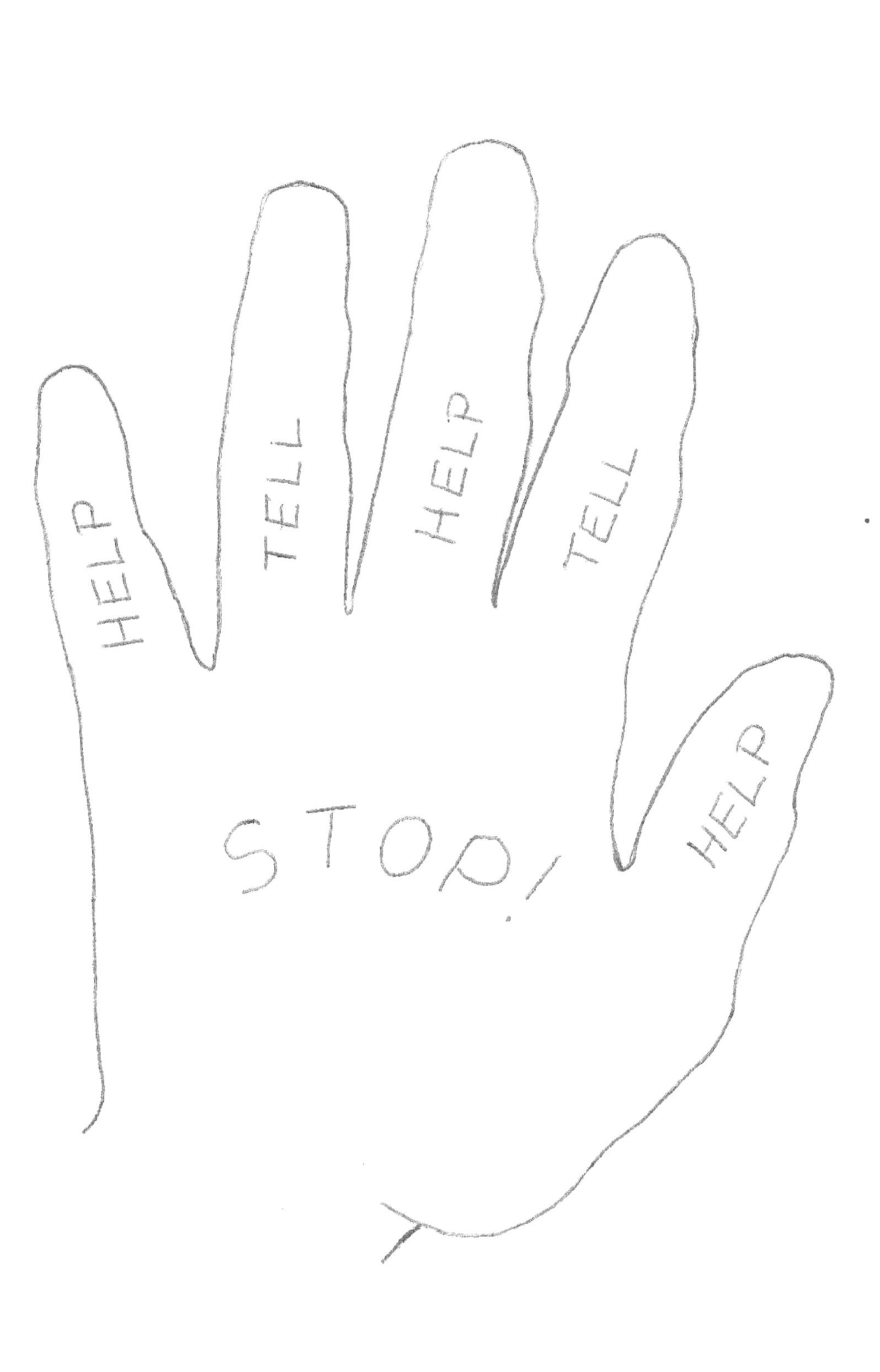

HELP
TELL
HELP
TELL
HELP
STOP!

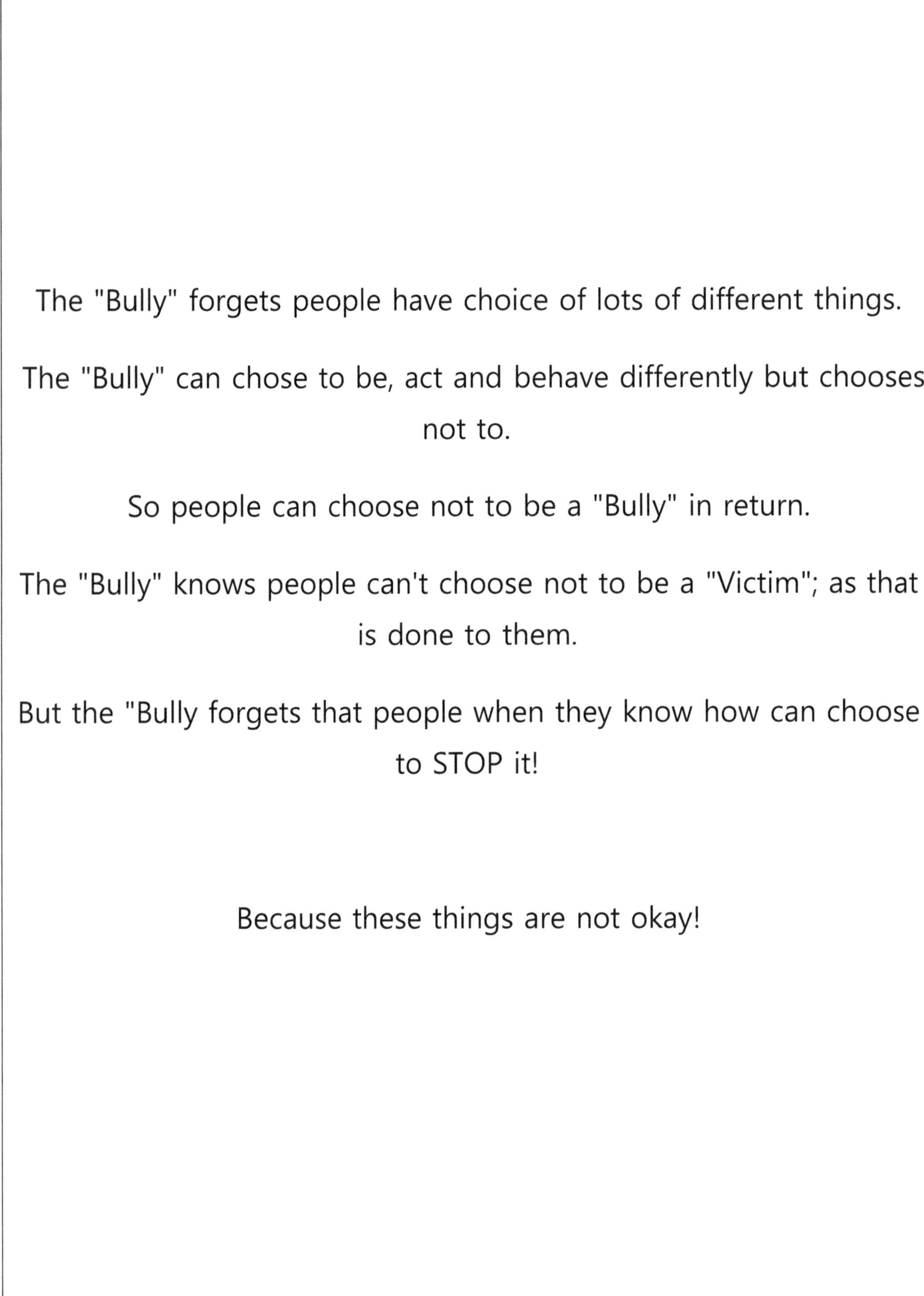

The "Bully" forgets people have choice of lots of different things.

The "Bully" can chose to be, act and behave differently but chooses not to.

So people can choose not to be a "Bully" in return.

The "Bully" knows people can't choose not to be a "Victim"; as that is done to them.

But the "Bully forgets that people when they know how can choose to STOP it!

Because these things are not okay!

Authors notes:

Remember another person's actions are never your fault.

Remember another person's violence or abuse is never your fault.

Remember the words that come out of people's mouth are their words not yours words and you do not have to own them.

Remember words are only words until you attach an emotion to it. Until you own the word and it's meaning.

Remember if you tell someone about the "Bully" and they do nothing, keep saying and telling until someone listens and does something. It's not okay to be bullied.

Remember you are an individual and that is a wonderfully great thing.

Remember that being "Bullied" is not okay and you do not need to put up with it, in any way.

If you have a "Bully" in your life these are the people who can help you: U.K. Help Organisations.

Childline 0800111

Police 101 or 999 emergency

National Bullying helpline 08452255787 or 07734701221

Bullying uk 08088002222

Kidscape 02078235430

Bully busters 08001696928

The Mix 0808084994

Ditch the label ditchthemabel.org

Cyber smile Foundation help@cybersmile.org

Samaritians 116123

Work place ACAS 03001231100

If you have a bully in your life. People: who can help could be:

Parent. Grandparent. Auntie and Uncles. Neighbour. Teacher.

Head teacher. SENCO. Friends parents.

If you have a bully in your life. Helping strangers who can help if you are out and about.

Police. Doctors. Health visitors. School Nurses. Children centre staff

Traffic warden. Road crossing person. Shop keepers. Security guards

Fire fighter.

ABOUT THE AUTHOR

Nettie Forsyth is a passionate advocate of Families, Children and Child development.

Known for her simplistic but vast knowledge base of Children, Child Development, Behaviour and Emotion work.

Nettie is appreciated by many she has worked with in her therapeutic behaviour strategy and now Counselling work.
Those who have had the privilege come away as very different people enabled and empowered.
The families functions and changes have been amazing within her work, whether it be child, siblings or parents.

Her Behaviour blogs and common sense to parenting has empowered many parents.

As a parent herself got thrown into Adoption issues, SEN and Aspergers which bought its own learning. This was used as a learning tool and gave Nettie more insight in to the world of Challenging Behaviour.

Her own Daughter becoming a successful young adult.
This all inspires the books she writes.

Contacts:

Challenging-Behaviour@hotmail.co.uk

www.help-with-challenging-behaviour.co.uk

Other books Written and Illustrated by the Author.
Loveall & Spike
Just being Crab
"These things are not Okay"

9 781722 917500